Fund-raising for your church building

A simple guide

2003–4

Church House Publishing
Church House
Great Smith Street
London SW1P 3NZ

ISBN 0 7151 7601 3

Published 2003 for the Council for the Care of Churches of the Church of England by Church House Publishing.

Typeset in 9pt Sabon

Cover design by Visible Edge

Printed by Halstan & Co. Ltd
Amersham, Bucks

Contents

Preface

This booklet aims to give simple, straightforward advice to parishes as to how they can raise money towards the cost of maintaining and developing their church building.

Church buildings are at one and the same time a joy, a delight, an opportunity and a challenge. They matter not just to the regular congregation but often to the wider community too. A major repair need, or a lack of facilities to do the work the church needs to do, can seem to be a burden. By engaging those many others who care about our buildings and what they can provide, the challenge becomes more manageable.

Every church is unique, so every appeal has to be tailored to suit the place. No guidance notes can cover every case so we have listed only those organizations that are in a position to make grants over the country as a whole, rather than those which are restricted to particular areas (apart from the county trusts).

Whatever your project, we wish you well in your endeavours to use and maintain your building for the mission of the Church and the service of the word.

Paula Griffiths
Head of Cathedral and Church Buildings Division

A request to fund-raisers

We hope that this guide has been of help to you. If you can suggest ways in which it may be made more useful please let us know. New ideas for fund-raising may well help other churches.

September 2003
Cathedral and Church Buildings Division
Church House, Great Smith Street, London SW1P 3NZ
Tel: 020 7898 1000; Fax: 020 7898 1881
Email: enquiries@ccc.c-of-e.org.uk

chapter 1
Funding

Churches and chapels, like other buildings, require regular maintenance and, from time to time, substantial repairs. These will often be beyond the immediate resources of the parish. This guide is designed to help you tackle the job of raising the money needed.

Raising money for fabric is sometimes regarded as a distraction from the 'real' work of the Church but experience shows that a well-run appeal is an opportunity for outreach and for bringing together different sections of the community. Many people are proud of 'their' church, even if they seldom enter it. They expect the church to be there, as a focus of that area and available for use when they want it. Such people may be prepared to help with a tangible project such as an appeal for the repair of the church building or the conservation of its historic furnishings.

Success depends on enthusiasm, hard work and persistence. Good organization and delegation will help to spread the load, whilst the information in this book will enable you to get the best out of the financial and other help that is available. It is also important that prayer is central to the appeal; that is the Church's *raison d'être*. An appeal prayer summing up the hopes of the venture will enable all to participate in the project, even if they have very little financially to contribute.

Why an appeal?

Quinquennial inspection report

Most fund-raising for the fabric, i.e. the structure of a church, starts with the arrival of the architect's or building surveyor's Quinquennial Inspection Report. The report will make clear what work is needed and what the priorities are. You cannot ignore the report – delay will only add to the cost, and the problems will not go away. The answer is to establish a plan of what to do and how to pay for it. If you are going to launch an appeal, it is better to aim at a comprehensive scheme of work that will see you through at least the next five years, rather than risk having to go back for more funds.

Your architect or surveyor will help you develop your strategy. It is essential at the outset to get from him or her a reasonably accurate idea of the cost of all the work you have in mind, including not only architect's and surveyor's fees and VAT but also associated aspects of the job, such as the Construction Design and Management regulations (CDM). If you are planning to apply to English Heritage for a grant towards the costs of the necessary works, it is important to bear in mind that the English Heritage has stipulated that from April 2003 grants will only be awarded to repair schemes carried out by accredited architects and surveyors. The Diocesan Archaeology Adviser will be able to give you a clear idea of the cost of any necessary archaeological work, contact your Diocesan Advisory Committee (DAC) Secretary for details. Estimates should assume the use of the best traditional methods and materials, unless your architect or surveyor recommends cheaper alternatives and has reason to believe that the DAC will be happy with them. The same principles apply to an appeal for the conservation of a particular element within the church such as the organ or the bells, or stained glass, wall-paintings or some other important object. The architect or surveyor should be invited to comment on a conservator's estimate and kept informed of the progress of the work.

Reordering schemes

The changing patterns of worship in the Church and the desire to use the building for a wider range of activities often lead parishes to think about reordering schemes. It is important that the archdeacon and the parish architect or surveyor are involved in any such discussions at an early stage. It is often useful to have an informal visit by members of the Diocesan Advisory Committee in order that the possibilities can be discussed before any formal plans are drawn up. In many instances English Heritage and one of the national amenity societies might also have an interest in the project.

Communicating such proposals to the congregation and the parish at large may not be easy. Some people may feel that to tamper with their church building means an attack on their very faith: others are so convinced of the necessity for change that they doubt the integrity of any opponent. It may therefore be helpful to have consultation sessions for those who may be interested in a project to come along and air their views at an early stage. Some simple before and after models or drawings could also help to explain changes.

Extensions/new building

Again, early consultation with interested parties will bring benefits in the long term. Discuss the proposals with English Heritage, the Council for the Care of Churches, the relevant amenity societies and the local planners in order that the process of obtaining a faculty will not be unnecessarily held up at a later stage. Be clear what the new extension will be used for and how it will benefit not just the church but the whole local community.

Appeal Committee

If the cost of work is very large and quite beyond the church's normal resources, it would be advisable to set up an Appeal Committee. However much you may dread another committee, a small group coordinating the appeal under a dynamic and efficient leader can be a real asset to any fund-raising initiative.

Not all members of the Appeal Committee have to be on the Parochial Church Council (PCC) or even the church electoral roll but it must be under the direction of the PCC. It is the PCC and not the Appeal Committee which has to give instructions to the architect or surveyor or builders, and which is legally responsible for any debts incurred. The choice of a good chairperson will be crucial. It is usually wiser if the incumbent is not the chairperson, but he or she should try to attend meetings.

It is important to draw members from wider sections of the community. Try to recruit people with financial skills. Is there someone who will be willing to take the minutes of the Appeal Committee meetings? The local historical society may like to be involved and to help promote the work amongst its membership. The parish school might wish to be linked to the project; an art competition in church will also bring parents to the launch. Someone should also be put in charge of publicity, organizing press releases and copy for the local newspaper and the diocesan newsletter. Appeal literature needs to be clearly worded and well laid out. For this reason, it is a great help if people with literary and artistic skills can be recruited to the Appeal Committee. There should be a well-designed letterhead and, if possible, a distinctive logo. Good photographs of the church will be of great help, especially when applying to grant-making bodies, so a keen photographer needs to be persuaded to give his or her services to the appeal.

Presenting your appeal

The appeal must be presented clearly so that people can give with confidence. What is special about your church? Why should individuals or companies or trusts dip into their pockets to help your appeal? How much is needed?

Take a fresh look at your church. Remind yourself of its architecture, its craftsmanship, its place in the landscape, and its place in the local community. Each of our churches is unique – even the most humble of our buildings has something special that can be brought out in an appeal letter. Do not underestimate the quality of the building, saying, 'it's only Victorian'! Even twentieth-century churches can be good examples of their type and will find admirers, helped by the growing appreciation of architecture of all periods.

It may be helpful to compile a 'Statement of Significance' and a 'Statement of Need' for your building at the start of your fund-raising drive. These documents, which set out to explain what is special about your church building and how any planned alternations to the building would meet the parish's needs, may be required later in the planning process in any case. Guidance on how to compile a Statement of Significance and a Statement of Need are available from the Council for the Care of Churches or by visiting www.churchcare.co.uk

Even if your appeal is a low-key affair, your paperwork can still stand out from others with very little effort. Grant-giving trusts complain that, on average, two out of three submissions from PCCs are inadequate. Typically, they fail to make clear:

- What the money is wanted for.
- When it is wanted.
- How much money is in hand or promised.

Sometimes the letters do not even state the location of the church concerned, which has to be guessed from the address of the correspondent! Not surprisingly, many grant-making trusts will simply reject applications where further research is needed, as they have neither the time nor the resources to fill in the gaps. Occasionally someone from a particular trust may want to visit the church to see that what is proposed is necessary or desirable.

It is possible to include too much information – pages of unnecessary background information may be well-meant but are difficult to plough through. The ideal is a short dossier of essential information, backed up by photographs or drawings where appropriate.

chapter 2
The appeal

It will be the job of the Appeal Committee, discussed on page 3, to plan and coordinate the launch of the appeal and to carry through the various fund-raising initiatives.

It is a good idea to set a time limit, for example, twelve months from the launch of the appeal. A small Cotswold parish raised a large sum in under a year. According to the appeal organizer: 'it is more practicable in our experience to go flat out for a defined time, than to struggle on over a long period, gradually losing momentum'. You should try to get the major part of the funds at least promised in the first few months of the appeal.

Launching the appeal

The Appeal Committee should produce a carefully-worded letter and/or leaflet to go to every household and business in the parish, explaining the scope of the appeal and giving details of a public launch meeting to be held in the near future. This letter should also be sent to people who used to live in the parish and to others who have links with the parish, e.g. those who were baptized or married in the church or whose family was buried there. Any leaflet should be attractive, concise and clear as to the aims of the appeal.

Experience shows that a launch works better if it is held a week or two after Easter until mid-June, or between early September and October half-term. It is probably better to hold the event in a public place rather than in a private home, as some people may be put off by this. The launch event could take a variety of forms but must be cheerful, fun, and positive in atmosphere. Short speeches (maximum five minutes!) may be made, setting out the nature of the appeal. If the expertise is available, a short video or slide presentation can be given, but again beware of excessive length. The event could be in the context of a special service or a major festival, or perhaps the stewardship supper approach may be used. Certainly refreshments should be provided, and of course budgeted for.

Who should you invite? An open invitation should be offered to everyone on the electoral roll along with other members of the church family. Local councillors, representatives of the local business community and possibly the rural dean and lay chair could also be invited to attend. Your initial leaflet drop to residents of the parish should also include an invitation.

Posters and graphs can be used to good advantage, by breaking down the overall target to a human scale, e.g. how the weekly equivalent of a newspaper or pint of beer will accumulate into large sums of money. It is vital that forms and information regarding tax-effective giving should be available, together with people who can explain what is involved (see www.inlandrevenue.gov.uk/charities for details). Where necessary, follow-up visits should be made as soon as possible after the launch, to encourage people to complete the necessary forms, or to answer any queries.

Fund-raising events

In most cases, there will be locally organized efforts, ranging from the familiar coffee morning through to more ambitious and imaginative sponsored events. Provided that the requirements are clearly understood in the parish, it is surprising how willingly subscribers and event organizers appear and offer their ideas. The important thing is that the Appeal Committee should carefully coordinate offers of help, so as to prevent repetition of events or a clash of dates.

The Appeal Committee should also examine the cost of proposed events in terms of financial outlay and organizational effort. The fund-raising committee may decide that any fund-raising event in their one-year programme must aim to raise at least £500, for example. A proposed pantomime may be ruled out because it would involve a great effort but would raise only a small amount of money.

There is no limit to the variety of events that can be organized. An auction has often proved successful, perhaps with a celebrity to conduct it. Proceeds might be divided fifty-fifty between the appeal and the donors of the objects being sold. Sponsored events of every description are usually popular, though not all are as imaginative as the cow-pat guessing game used by one appeal. Part of a field was marked out in squares, and a cow was borrowed for the occasion. Sponsors selected one or more squares, the first to be marked (in obvious fashion) being the winner! In another parish a lady persuaded her husband to let her take B&B guests and, after a year, was able to contribute £1,000 to the appeal.

Gift Day

Many parishes have found that a specific Gift Day marks a useful starting point to a fund-raising campaign. It is likely that this will happen on a day perhaps halfway through the appeal, in order to keep the momentum going.

Local businesses

It has already been suggested that the launch letter should go to businesses as well as individuals living in or beyond the parish. Your district council should be able to provide a list of local firms; alternatively you will find various directories at the main reference libraries. Write to the managing director or the company secretary, preferably by name. Indeed, a member of the congregation may know a senior member of staff and could deliver it by hand.

You may find it helpful to ask for a specific amount, rather than making an open-ended appeal for 'any contribution, large or small'. For a local business that does not normally give money to church repairs, it is easier to make a decision as to whether or not to respond to your appeal if a reasonable figure is suggested in your letter. This approach usually ensures that the sum sent, if any, is generally the figure suggested. Some parishes have held a function especially for local business people. A lunchtime event has proven successful where this has been undertaken.

Firms unwilling to give directly to the Appeal may agree to sponsor an event, or to fund a leaflet, because of the publicity that they will receive. They may also be prepared to give gifts in kind. You should always discuss this with your architect and possibly Diocesan Advisory Committee secretary. Make use of any local contacts you may have, such as the Chamber of Commerce.

Marketing promotions

Many firms will provide suitably inscribed goods such as mugs, tee shirts, Christmas cards, etc. The initial cost can be high, and you should look closely at the likely sales and eventual profit. Be very wary of 'dated' goods such as calendars or diaries. Obviously these are valueless once they are out of date. The Charity Commission is quite cautious about charitable funds being put at risk by charitable trading and the Appeal Committee should be aware of this. Specific queries should be addressed to the Charity Commissioners whose address and telephone number are listed under Appendix 2.

Professional fund-raisers

Professionals may have their place in a very large appeal, but are probably not worthwhile for the medium or smaller appeal. Their fees and expenses must be paid from money raised, regardless of how much their efforts bring in (although some fund-raisers charge a percentage of the money raised rather than a flat fee). Most such professionals will be unwilling to consider an appeal intended to raise less than £500,000.

Stewardship department

On the other hand, the Diocesan Stewardship Adviser will be pleased to help. Other officers at the diocesan office may be able to help with advice about the financial or legal aspects of fund-raising. They are often also able to advise on specific issues regarding fund-raising and appeals and in some instances may be able to help in the filling out of forms or by guiding you in the right direction for grants.

chapter 3

Loan finance

It may be worth taking out loans to enable work to proceed in one continuous operation, whilst fund-raising is going on. Obviously this will be dependent on the ability of the parish to cope with the burden of repayment.

Once the project work has been paid for by means of a loan, much of the impetus for fund-raising will have been lost and it will not be easy to win support to pay off the loan, not to mention the interest. This could result in a parish becoming saddled with a debt over a long period. It is wise therefore to maintain the momentum of the appeal and to keep the use of loans to a minimum. It is also worth remembering that many grant-giving agencies (including English Heritage and the Heritage Lottery Fund) will not grant-aid work that has already been completed.

ICBS loans

The Incorporated Church Building Society (Fulham Palace, London SW6 6EA) makes interest-free loans, irrespective of the architectural grading of the building.

Diocesan loans

Many Diocesan Boards of Finance offer loans in respect of repairs to church fabric, reordering or for new buildings. You should approach your diocesan office to see whether they offer such a facility (see also Chapter 5).

Loans from individuals

Some individuals may wish to make a loan to the appeal. This may be for part of the whole or a specific project. Their contribution to the appeal is the loss of interest that they incur. The diocesan registrar will usually be pleased to draw up any contract needed.

chapter 4

The major grant givers

English Heritage and the Heritage Lottery Fund

Few parishes can raise enough money to meet the cost of a major repair without help from grant-making bodies. The major source in England is now likely to be the Repair Grants for Places of Worship in England scheme run by English Heritage (EH) and the Heritage Lottery Fund (HLF), and funded in equal proportion by both bodies.

This scheme is jointly funded by the HLF and EH and gives grants for urgent repairs to listed buildings which are in regular use as a place of worship (excluding cathedrals). All faith groups and denominations, Christian and non-Christian, are eligible to apply as long as they are a formally constituted religious organization. The scheme operates on an annual batch basis, with closing dates for applications in June and September.

The main focus of the scheme is to support urgent repairs required to high-level features such as roofs, towers, spires and associated masonry although other urgent repair work can be considered if there is an imminent threat to the historic fabric. The scheme may also assist with professional fees and VAT that cannot be reclaimed under the Listed Places of Worship Grant Scheme (see page 14).

Priority will be given to single repair projects costing less than £200,000 (including fees and VAT), normally to be carried out in a single contract. Successful applicants will be expected to prepare and implement a long-term maintenance plan for their place of worship and provide a guaranteed level of visitor access to the building outside the usual hours of worship. Grants cannot be considered for new work, alterations, minor repairs, or improvements to community facilities within the place of worship.

The scheme may make a grant provided:

1. The building is listed at Grade I, II* or II. If you need to know if your church is listed contact your District Council Planning Department, or the Diocesan Office.

2. The church is used for public worship on at least six days a year and is open to the public outside the normal hours of worship.

3. The grant will be used to pay for high-level structural repairs (e.g. repair of roofs, towers, spires, rainwater disposal systems or high-level masonry) identified in a recent condition survey as being necessary within the next two years.

4. The work will cost more than £10,000 and less than £200,000 and can be carried out under one contract.

Grants are never made retrospectively for work started before the application has been approved.

Although grant offers will be made from the Heritage Lottery Fund and English Heritage, the day-to-day administration of the scheme is carried out by English Heritage regional offices on behalf of both organizations. Full details of the scheme and an application pack can be obtained from the English Heritage website www.english-heritage.org.uk or by contacting English Heritage Customer Services department on 0870 333 1181 (email: customers@english-heritage.org.uk).

Contact:
English Heritage
23 Saville Row
London W1S 2ET
Tel: 020 7973 3267
Web site: english-heritage.org.uk

Heritage Lottery Fund 'Your Heritage' scheme

The Heritage Lottery Fund 'Your Heritage' scheme can consider applications for conservation of historic furnishings and works of art in places of worship. This programme offers grants to organizations which aim to look after and enhance the UK's heritage, to increase involvement in heritage activities and to improve access to and enjoyment of heritage. Under the *Your Heritage* scheme grants of £5,000 to £50,000 can be awarded, although the total project cost can exceed £50,000. The scheme aims to achieve a twelve-week turnaround of grant applications. Projects must be able to demonstrate educational and community benefits and applicants must ensure that their premises are accessible to visitors. At the CCC's initiative, the HLF have agreed to include conservation projects in churches relating to bells, clocks, organs, paintings on canvas and wood, wall-paintings, monuments, timberwork, ornamental plasterwork, metalwork, books and manuscripts, and textiles, as well as historic structures and other conservation projects in churchyards.

Contact:
Head Office
Heritage Lottery Fund
7 Holbein Place
London SW1H 8NR
Tel: 020 7591 6042
Web site: www.hlf.org.uk

The ethical aspect of applying for Lottery money

Some parishes may question whether they should have anything to do with the National Lottery. Each parish is free to make its own decision. The policy agreed nationally by the House of Bishops is as follows:

> Throughout the debate on the establishment of the National Lottery, the Church of England, along with other churches, has made known its reservations. We accept freely our own financial responsibility in worship, witness, evangelism and pastoral care, and see no basis on which Lottery money should be used by the Church in these areas.
>
> However, it is clearly the Government's intention that the Church's heritage responsibilities should attract grants from public funds made available through the Lottery.
>
> Sometimes the Church resists proposed changes in our society, but when the decision is made we have to live with it. In this instance we recognize that the Government has made it clear that the Lottery is the way it will increasingly fund heritage and charitable and other matters.

If a parish decides not to seek Lottery funding on moral grounds, this should be indicated on the application form and supported by the relevant PCC resolution. Any grant will then be offered from English Heritage alone. EH's remit is more restricted than that of the HLF and you should check before applying that you are eligible for EH help.

Listed Places of Worship Grant Scheme

In his Budget in March 2001, the Chancellor announced the establishment of a new UK-wide grant scheme, the effect of which will be to reduce the VAT cost to 5 per cent for repair work to listed churches started after 1 April 2001. The Listed Places of Worship Grant Scheme (LPWS) is an interim measure until the Government is able to secure a permanent reduced rate of VAT for these repairs through the European Commission. However, the scheme is currently set to run until at least March 2004.

The LPWS applies to all listed places of worship, of all religions throughout the UK, used for worship at least six times a year. It allows parishes to claim back the equivalent of 12.5 per cent VAT on repair works carried out by a registered VAT contractor, effectively reducing the rate of VAT paid to 5 per cent. It is important to note that the full rate of VAT needs to be paid before you can claim the money back. For example:

A parish has carried out repairs costing £1,000. VAT is charged by the contractor at the usual rate of 17.5 per cent giving a total bill of £1,175. After paying the bill, the parish applies to the LPWS and gets a refund of 12.5 per cent of the cost of the repairs. In this case, the £1,000 bill for the repairs would enable the parish to claim £125 back. The work will therefore cost the parish £1,050 in total which is equivalent to VAT rate of 5 per cent.

For full details of this scheme and an application form visit www.lpwscheme.org.uk, phone 0845 601 5945 or write to
Listed Places of Worship Grant Scheme
PO Box 609
Newport NP10 8QD

Bodies in other parts of the United Kingdom

In Wales, Scotland and Northern Ireland there are comparable but not identical schemes to that of English Heritage. The grants are administered by:

CADW (Welsh Historic Monuments)

Brunel House
Fitzalan Road
Cardiff CF2 1UY
Tel: 01222 825111
Web site: www.cadw.wales.gov.uk

Historic Scotland

Scottish Development Department
Perth Street
Edinburgh EH3 5RB
Tel: 0131 668 8600
Web site: www.historic-scotland.gov.uk

Northern Ireland Office

Historic Monuments and Buildings Branch
Calvert House
Castle Place
Belfast BT1 1FY
Tel: 028 9023 5000
Web site: www.nio.gov.uk

These bodies can advise on sources of grant-aid particular to their areas. The HLF however can give grants in all parts of the United Kingdom.

Other Lottery funds

The Arts Council

The Arts Lottery Fund, administered by the Arts Council, may be of assistance for churches seeking to improve their cultural facilities, e.g. use for concerts, plays etc. and to commission contemporary art and craft work. It may also assist major organ reconstruction projects for concert use (although for the conservation of historic instruments, application should be made to the Heritage Lottery Fund). It is advisable to discuss any possible application beforehand with your Regional Art Board.

Contact:
Arts Council of England
Lottery Department
14 Great Peter Street
London SW1P 3NQ
Tel: 020 7312 0123
Web site: www.artscouncil.org.uk

The Community Fund

The Community Fund distributes a share of the money raised by the National Lottery to support charitable, benevolent and philanthropic organizations throughout the UK. It cannot fund repair works but can give grants towards community projects in churches, for example refurbishing a meeting room.

Contact:
The Community Fund
St Vincent House
16 Suffolk Street
London SW1Y 4NL
Tel: 020 7747 5299
Email: enquiries@community-fund.org.uk
Web site: www.c-f.org.uk

The Foundation for Sport and the Arts

This trust was set up in order to distribute funds awarded to it by the football pools companies from their profits. The money available has therefore been severely reduced by the impact of the National Lottery on the pools. The Foundation will require you to establish that your project has significant community benefit. In the past they have made grants towards the restoration of historic organs where the instrument is used for public concerts.

Contact:
The Foundation for Sport and the Arts
PO Box 20
Liverpool L13 1HB
Tel: 0151 259 5505

Landfill Tax Credit Scheme

The Landfill Tax Credit Scheme (LTCS) was designed to help mitigate the effects of landfill upon local communities and support moves to more sustainable waste management practices. It encourages partnerships between landfill operators, their local communities and the voluntary and public sectors. Since 1996 landfill operators have been permitted to offset up to 20 per cent of their tax obligations as a credit that can be applied to environmental bodies and projects which can include the maintenance and repair of church buildings whether listed or not. The regulatory body of the Landfill Tax Credit Scheme is Entrust, from whom an information pack is available. A list of local contractors should be available from your local authority. Some local councils and dioceses have already enrolled themselves and local projects can therefore benefit from this. You should check with the relevant local authority and with your diocese. The Government has recently changed the regulations governing the LTCS so that more money is available for initiatives to encourage sustainable waste management. This may mean that less money is available for projects such as repairing a church building.

Contact:
Entrust
Suite 2
5th Floor Acre House
2 Town Square
Sale
Cheshire M33 7WZ
Tel: 0161 972 0044
Web site: www.entrust.org.uk

Aggregates Levy Sustainability Fund

A similar scheme to the Landfill Tax Credit Scheme, the Aggregates Levy Sustainability Fund, seeks to address quarrying's impact on the environment in three ways: by improving existing sites, by reducing the need for new quarrying and by making any new quarrying more sensitive. Some parishes have been successful in getting grants from this fund for various purposes. Money is distributed by three agencies:

- English Heritage – for historic landscape, generally archaeological, projects. Tel: 020 7973 3120.

- English Nature – for projects for ecological and biodiversity benefits. Tel: 01392 889777.
- Countryside Agency – for projects with landscape, community and recreational benefits. Tel: 0117 970 7924.

chapter 5

Grant-aid from other sources

General points on applying

The process of obtaining and completing all the necessary forms can seem daunting. A certain amount of coordination and persistence is required, so the job needs to be done by someone who is used to dealing with paperwork.

Several points should be borne in mind when drafting letters to grant-making bodies.

1. The small cost of enclosing a stamped addressed envelope with appeal letters is a worthwhile courtesy. It is appreciated by hard-pressed charities.
2. The appeal letter should be carefully and clearly drafted. The purpose of the appeal and the extent of local effort should come across. The recipient should be quite clear that the parish is not expecting others to solve its problems by handouts.
3. When putting together your application, make sure you have given all the necessary information, but without going into excessive detail. Remember that your application will be one of many to be considered by the relevant committee or the trustees of the charity. A few good photographs are of great help as a back-up.
4. Look again at the advice on presentation in Chapter 1.

Local authorities

The Local Authority (Historic Buildings) Act 1962 and Planning (Listed Buildings and Conservation Areas) Act 1990 permit a local authority (whether at county, district or parish council level) to contribute by grant or loan towards the maintenance or repair of historic buildings in its area, including churches. Given pressure on local authority funds, you may find it helpful to stress that your building is also a cultural asset and/or a tourist attraction within the area. Enquiries should be addressed to the planning officer concerned.

Parish councils (which are often responsible legally for carrying out maintenance to closed churchyards) may be prepared to make an annual grant towards the upkeep of open churchyards and, given sufficient prior warning for budgeting purposes, may be able to provide a grant for maintenance of the church building itself.

Diocesan grants

Most dioceses can give modest grants and/or interest-free loans for the repair of their churches. Several have savings schemes to which you may contribute and from whose funds you may borrow. Application should be made to the Secretary of the Diocesan Board of Finance or the Church Buildings Committee at the diocesan office. (Details of these funds are generally published in the Diocesan Handbook.) The diocesan office may also be able to provide information regarding any local charitable funds.

Grant-making trusts: how to find the right one

The major source for identifying suitable trusts is the *Directory of Grant Making Trusts*, published by the Charities Aid Foundation, King's Hill, West Malling, Kent, ME19 4TA. It is available at main public reference libraries. The Directory lists a large number of organizations that may accept applications for grant-aid, states their relevant criteria, and indicates the approximate annual income of each charity. It also contains important advice on how to present your applications. You are advised to read this very carefully and be guided by it. It is now also available on CD-ROM. The Directory is updated twice yearly. Some dioceses have a copy of the Directory that they are prepared to let parishes borrow; it may be worth while asking.

Be ready for a high proportion of disappointing replies. It pays to be persistent however; the last trust on your list could be one that is willing to help you.

If you have access to the Internet, the Charity Commissioners web site includes the Register of Charities, which can be browsed and used to highlight trusts by name, object, or area of benefit. This can be accessed via www.charity-commission.gov.uk

Grants for fabric repairs

The following organizations give grants towards general fabric repairs. Some of them exclude decoration, lighting/heating, improvements and other work that is not seen as essential maintenance of the fabric.

The Historic Churches Preservation Trust (HCPT)

Fulham Palace
London SW6 6EA
Tel: 020 7736 3054

Churches must be over 100 years old to qualify for grant-aid. Interest-free loans are also made. The maximum grant or loan is usually £6,000. Where a church is in principle eligible for English Heritage or Heritage Lottery Fund grant-aid (see chapter 4) the HCPT will expect an application to have been made, and will want to know the outcome. Only repairs to the fabric will be considered.

The Diocesan Advisory Committee will be asked for its comments by the HCPT. Grants are not made for work that has been started or has already been completed.

The Incorporated Church Building Society (ICBS)

The ICBS is now administered by the Historic Churches Preservation Trust (see above) and can be contacted at the same address and telephone number.

The ICBS gives interest-free loans and some grants to Anglican churches only. Conditions are similar to the HCPT, except that the ICBS can also assist churches in Wales and churches less than 100 years old.

The Chase Charity

c/o 2 The Court
High Street
Harwell
Didcot OX11 OEY
Tel: 01235 820044

The Chase Charity makes a dozen or so grants to ancient churches each year, concentrating on the repair of rural parish churches. The trustees say that they are more likely to be sympathetic to unforeseen crises, rather than to general repair appeals. The building must be Grade I listed in a village of under 500 people and the local community must support the appeal. Grants range in size from £1,000 to £3,000.

The Sainsbury Family Trusts

Allington House 1st floor
150 Victoria Street
London SW1E 5AE
Tel: 020 7410 0330

There are a number of Sainsbury Family Charitable Trusts, several of which, particularly the Monument Historic Buildings Trust, grant-aid church repair work. One letter (about two sides of A4) to the address above will ensure that an appeal is considered by whichever of the trusts is the most appropriate.

The Garfield Weston Foundation

Weston Centre
Bowater House
68 Knightsbridge
London SW1X 7LR
Tel: 020 7589 6363

The foundation is prepared to consider general church fabric appeals.

County Historic Churches Trusts

There are now 32 County Churches Trusts that give grants to places of worship of all denominations in their own county; a list is appended (see Appendix 3). You should, of course, only apply to the county trust relevant to your area. A county trust cannot offer grants outside its own boundaries.

Conservation of furnishings and fittings

Council for the Care of Churches

Conservation Officer: Andrew Argyrakis
Church House
Great Smith Street
London SW1P 3NZ
Tel: 020 7898 1885
Fax: 020 7898 1881
Email: enquiries@ccc.c-of-e.org.uk

The Council for the Care of Churches (CCC) administers funds for the conservation of church furnishings of particular historic and/or artistic importance, e.g. clocks, bells, textiles, wall-paintings, paintings on wood and canvas, metalwork, stained glass and monuments, and for historic structures in churchyards. These grants are available to churches of all denominations in England, Wales and Scotland. The principal contributors to these funds are the Pilgrim Trust and the Esmée Fairbairn Charitable Trust.

Applications made direct to these Trusts are automatically forwarded to the Council for the Care of Churches.

The Council also distributes the Rupert Gunnis Memorial Fund for the conservation of important English monuments built between 1680 and 1840.

Through the generosity of the Wolfson Foundation some funds are also available for fabric repair to Anglican churches in England, Scotland and Wales that are listed Grade I, or exceptionally Grade II*, and were built before 1850.

The Leche Trust

Secretary: Mrs Louisa Lawson
84 Cicada Road
London SW18 2NZ
Tel: 020 8870 6233

The Leche Trust assists conservation of furnishings and fittings within the period 1680 to 1830.

The Manifold Trust

Sir John Smith CH CBE
Shottesbrooke House
Maidenhead SL6 2SW

The Manifold Trust assists with conservation of furnishings and fittings.

The Morris Bequest

c/o The General Secretary
Society of Antiquaries, Burlington House
Piccadilly
London W1V OHS
Tel: 020 7734 0193

Preference is given to limited programmes of work connected with conservation of decoration, stained glass, sculpture, monuments and tombs. Grants are allocated annually, and application forms must be submitted by 31 August in any year.

Bells

The Barron Bell Trust

I. H. Walrond
71 Lower Green Road
Pembury
Tunbridge Wells TN2 4EB

Applicants should have raised in the region of 50 per cent of the total cost of the project prior to application. The Trustees state that they will not consider applications from 'high church' parishes.

The Sharpe Trust

c/o The Grant Secretary
Mr A. Strickland
71 North Holme Road
Cirencester GL7 1DA

Applications should be addressed to the Grant Secretary in writing.

The Central Council of Church Bell Ringers

c/o Mr I. H. Oram
The Cottage
School Hill
Warnham
Horsham
West Sussex RH12 3QN
Web site: www.cccbr.org.uk

The Council for the Care of Churches can offer some grant-aid towards the conservation of historic or important bells.

Organs

The Arts Council Arts Lottery Fund

Organ appeals in connection with concert and other performances should approach the Arts Lottery Fund. The Heritage Lottery Fund *Your Heritage* scheme may be appropriate for major works to historic instruments.

The O N Organ Fund
36 Strode Road
Forest Gate
London E7 0DU
Tel: 020 8555 4391

Grant assistance for organ repairs – national coverage.

The Council for the Care of Churches will consider grant-aid for repairs to organs of outstanding artistic or historical interest.

The Manifold Trust will consider applications for organs.

The Ouseley Trust
Mr Martin Williams
127 Coleherne Court
Old Brompton Road
London SW5 0EB
Tel: 020 7373 1950
Email: clerk@ouseleytrust.org.uk

Funding is available for organ repairs and other musical objects for churches where there is an active choral tradition.

The Foundation for Sport and The Arts
P O Box 20
Liverpool L1 1HB
Tel: 0151 259 5505

The Pilling Trust
Waterworths
Central Buildings
Richmond Terrace
Blackburn
Lancashire BB1 7AP

The Pilling Trust is particularly interested in churches that maintain an active choral tradition. They will consider new organs and electronic instruments.

The British Institute of Organ Studies (BIOS) has produced a leaflet *A Guide to Grants for Funding Work on Historic Pipe Organs*. This gives details of charities that have made grants towards the conservation of historic organs. It also gives useful information about the preparation of organ appeals and how to research the history of your instruments. This guide is available at www.bios.org.uk

The Honorary Secretary
British Institute of Organ Studies
Lime Tree Cottage
39 Church Street
Haslingfield
Cambridge CB3 7JE

Significant tombs in churchyards and churchyard furnishings

District councils are empowered to give grants. The CCC also has some funds available for conserving important churchyard monuments (see pages 22-3). Contact the CCC's Conservation Officer for further details. For Georgian tombs try the Leche Trust (see page 23).

The Livery Companies

The Livery Companies of the City of London have funds for charitable works, but they vary greatly in their resources. Applications most likely to be successful are for work to be carried out on items of specific interest to that Company, e.g. the Worshipful Company of Glaziers for the conservation of stained glass, or for parishes in areas connected with a Company, e.g. the Tonbridge area of Kent and the Skinners' Company.

Applications should be addressed to The Clerk. A list of the companies and their addresses is given in *Whittaker's Almanack* and also in the *City of London Directory and Livery Companies Guide*.

Regional or local trusts

There are many trusts that will assist churches in particular areas. Consult the *Directory of Grant Making Trusts* or staff in your diocesan office. The Charity Commission web site allows you to browse the Register of Charities using criteria such as location and keywords (www.charity.commission.gov.uk). Some charities may not be on the Register and it might therefore be useful to ask around locally, for example, at the Citizens' Advice Bureaux, or with firms of long-established solicitors.

chapter 6

Longer-term funding for repairs

There are those who feel that it is poor stewardship to wait until the needs of the fabric can be ignored no longer and then to launch a big public appeal. Should we do more to provide for future maintenance, to stave off the crisis before it happens?

In particular it is sensible to consider how the burden of maintaining the fabric might be spread beyond the PCC and the regular church-goers.

1. The Perpetual Fabric Fund

The idea of a Perpetual Fabric Fund (PFF) is to provide a capital fund to which anyone can contribute in the knowledge that their money can only be spent on the fabric of the church concerned. It is an arrangement which may attract substantial gifts or legacies from non-church-goers – people who are reluctant to contribute to general PCC funds, but who are willing to support the bricks and mortar of a particular church.

There are now a number of these funds in operation. Further details should be available from the diocesan office.

2. Friends organization

Another approach is to create a 'Friends' group – people who do not necessarily worship in the church on a regular basis but are anxious that the building be maintained. Subscriptions from the 'Friends' can be used to maintain the building and fabric. Members of 'Friends' organizations can in time be drawn more fully into supporting the life and worship of the church. The Diocese of Canterbury produces an excellent book called *A Friends Scheme for a Parish Church* (cost £3.50 and available from the Stewardship Adviser at Diocesan House, Canterbury, Kent, CT1 2EE. Tel: 01227 459401).

'Friends' organizations can be either under the umbrella of the PCC or registered as a separate charity. The organization can make a grant of funds to the PCC in order that the elected representatives of the congregation have responsibility for spending this without restriction. It is always useful to discuss the proposed trust deed with the Charity Commission, as well as the local diocese.

3. **Diocesan church repair fund**

   The Diocese of Rochester operates a system whereby the inspecting architect, producing the Quinquennial Inspection Report, gives an estimate of the anticipated cost of repairs in five years' time. After the addition of an allowance for inflation, an annual sum is then notified to the PCC and it is suggested that the amount be paid over the five-year period into a fund held by the diocese. Interest is added and when the next QI report is produced this money is made available to the PCC to meet the cost of immediate repairs. Contact your diocesan office to discuss such a scheme.

chapter 7

Looking after the fabric

Once your repairs have been done – don't stop! The church fabric will always require attention sooner or later.

Dilapidation can be accelerated drastically by lack of attention to basics. In particular, gutters, downpipes and drains can do much damage if they become blocked or broken. By concentrating waste water into a few areas, they can prove worse than useless, and this is why they should be checked and cleared at least once a year after leaf fall.

If your PCC lacks the access equipment or the able-bodied personnel willing to carry out this work, you are strongly advised to find a competent and trustworthy local builder to check and clear gullies and rainwater goods once or twice a year. Your architect or surveyor may be able to recommend a suitable firm. If this job is done properly, many minor defects can be nipped in the bud and a great deal of money saved thereby.

Well-meant but ignorant DIY work and the use of modern materials that are not suitable for ancient fabric can cause damage. For instance, the use of modern hard cement for repointing can do much damage to the stone that it was intended to protect.

Church maintenance should not be left to chance. Each PCC must maintain a Church Log Book, blank copies of which are obtainable from the Church House Bookshop, Great Smith Street, London SW1P 3BN (tel: 020 7898 1300, web site: www.chbookshop.co.uk). This is of great assistance to your architect or surveyor and will help you to put church maintenance on to a disciplined and regular basis. The Council for the Care of Churches produces a range of publications on all aspects of caring for a church building, all of which are available from Church House Bookshop. The CCC also maintains a web site giving practical information on caring for church buildings at www. churchcare.co.uk

By sensible and consistent maintenance, further fund-raising efforts may be staved off for many years to come.

chapter 8

Adaptations and reordering

There is not space in this guide to enter into a detailed discussion about making changes to your church. This is a wide-ranging and complex area, and the casework keeps the Diocesan Advisory Committees very busy. The CCC publishes a useful book on the subject: *Church Extensions and Adaptations*, £9.95 from Church House Bookshop. This includes a chapter on the financial aspects, including fund-raising. If you are planning works to improve access to your building, the CCC's book *Widening the Eye of the Needle* (£10.95 from Church House Bookshop) would prove very useful.

Many organizations that give assistance for repairs to churches are unable to consider improvement projects. A notable exception is the Heritage Lottery Fund, which may be able to consider projects for providing new facilities where it can be demonstrated that the works are essential to secure wider use of the building and will benefit the wider community.

These works largely fall outside the scope of this guide. The grant-making bodies that traditionally assist with church restoration and conservation work are mostly unable to direct their funds to new capital projects as well.

However, organizations that may make grants or loans for new works include the following:

The Incorporated Church Building Society

Fulham Palace
London SW6 6EA

The ICBS makes interest-free loans available.

Central Church Fund

Among a wide variety of objects, grants are made for adaptation of church buildings for wider community use. The maximum grant is £10,000, but most grants are around £5,000. Contact the Secretary at:

Church House
Great Smith Street
London SW1P 3NZ
Tel: 020 7898 1563

Church Urban Fund

To qualify for funding, parishes must have an 'OXLIP' score of greater than 19, or comprise areas of significant deprivation. Contact the Church Urban Fund at:
1 Millbank
London SW1P 3JZ
Tel: 020 7898 1729

Local authorities

Contact should be made with the Social Services Department of the County Council for building works connected with care projects. The relevant district or borough council should also be approached for help.

The Chase Charity

c/o The Court
High Street
Harwell
Didcot OX11 0EY
Tel: 01235 820044

Of particular interest to the trustees are projects connected with community development in rural areas and youth unemployment. One-off grants of up to £3,000 are the norm.

The National Lottery

The Heritage Lottery Fund may consider schemes that enhance the amenities of a listed building. The Arts Council may assist schemes directly related to promotion of artistic activities at a church, e.g. demountable staging, improved lavatories, etc.

Please note that there are other charitable organizations not included in this list which may consider making grants for specific projects. For further details refer to *The Directory of Grant Making Trusts.*

Disabled access

Disabled access is increasingly of importance to those who care for church buildings. The first two parts of the Disability Discrimination Act (DDA) have been implemented. Part three, which may require 'reasonable adjustment' to physical features to overcome barriers to enable disabled worshippers to have, within reason, the same opportunities as able-bodied people, will be implemented in 2004. Currently there is no central fund from which help is available for such works. Local authorities may be able to point out possible sources of funding. The Central Church Fund may be able to contribute to the cost of such work if it is part of a larger programme of work.

appendix 1

The amazing mailshot

Case study showing the success of an imaginative, specifically targeted style of appeal coupled with systematic research and administration. (Reproduced by permission.)

CHURCH TIMES

'Amazing' mailshot saves church

THE FUND-RAISING STRATEGY of a west London parish church has won it two Direct Marketing Industry awards for cost-effectiveness (£744 raised for every £1 spent), and for its use of databases. The strategy was devised for the St James Norlands restoration appeal by two parishioners, Pam Craik and Jon Voelkel, who raised £150,000 with one accurately targeted mailshot. Ninety per cent of donors had never given to the church before.

'We are simply amazed at the church's achievement' said the chairman of the awards committee, Fabienne Tyler. 'These awards are the Oscars of the direct-marketing world.'

St James Norlands, a Grade II listed 19th-century church in gardens in the centre of a square, had been threatened with closure, and needed £300,000 for its rescue plan. The object of the mailshot was to raise the first half of this.

The fund-raisers compiled a database that segmented the parish by wealth (based on the value of houses and flats), location, and by each person's use of the church. Parishioners received emotive letters, slightly differently angled to reflect the recipients' interests and values, but all with the reminder that 'St James Norlands is as much part of this neighbourhood as the squirrels in the park or the shops on Holland Park Avenue.'

Each recipient's point of leverage was carefully judged. To those living in the square, in houses valued at over £1 million, the fund-raisers wrote: 'How sad would be the prospect if St James's were forced to close, if its White Suffolk bricks were scrawled with graffiti and its 22 stained-glass windows were all boarded up. Or if it were redeveloped as a block of flats.'

Parents of children baptised there received letters beginning: 'If you remember that very special day when Francesca was baptised at St James's ...'

Celebrities were approached individually: Elton John, for instance, received a letter from the organist, rhapsodising about the organ's sound ('riproaring good fun'), and inviting him to 'sneak away one summer's evening and come and put the organ through its paces'. (But Elton John gives only to AIDS charities, he says.)

The Vicar, the Revd Hugh Rayment-Pickard, said that the parish was thrilled by the awards. 'We didn't realise we were direct marketing: we were just trying to save the church.'

Plans for its future include a nursery centre for small children, and the use of the church for concerts and opera in the evenings.

appendix 2

Bibliography

The following two leaflets are available from Church House Bookshop, Church House, Great Smith Street, London SW1P 3BN, Tel: 020 7898 1306 or at www.chbookshop.co.uk

Receiving and Giving: The Basis, Issues and Implications of Christian Stewardship, General Synod Report GS 943.

Guide to Giving by Gift Aid – Guidance notes for officers of Parochial Church Councils, Stewardship, or Finance Committee members, and incumbents, Achbishops' Council, 2000.

Other useful publications might include:

Church Extensions and Adaptations, Church House Publishing, 2001.

A Guide to Church Inspection and Repair, Church House Publishing, 2003.

Widening the Eye of the Needle, Church House Publishing, 2001.

Fundraising for Churches, Jane Grieve, 1999, SPCK.

The Charity Commissioners for England and Wales, St. Albans House, 57–60 Haymarket, London SW1Y 4QX (tel: 020 7210 4556) produce various publications which might be useful in parish finances. These include:

Charity Reserves (CC19), Charity Commission, 1999.

Use of Church Halls for Village Hall and Other Charitable Purposes (CC18), Charity Commission, 1996.

Many of the publications of the Charity Commission are available on their web site: www.charity-commission.gov.uk

Further information on all aspects of caring for church buildings can be found at www.churchcare.co.uk

appendix 3

County trusts

(NB only apply to the county trust for the county in which your church is situated)

Bedfordshire
Mr R. Tomlins
Bedfordshire and Hertfordshire
Historic Churches Trust
80 Beaumont Avenue
St Albans
Hertfordshire AL1 4TP

Berkshire
Mrs Jan Viger
Royal County of Berkshire
Churches Trust
The Briars
53 Rose Hill
Binfield
Berkshire RG42 5LH

Buckinghamshire
Sir Henry Aubrey-Fletcher Bt
Buckinghamshire Historic
Churches Trust
Townhill Farm
Chilton
Aylesbury
Buckinghamshire HP18 9LR

Cambridgeshire
Mr J. N. Cleaver
Cambridgeshire Historic
Churches Trust
14 High Street
Histon
Cambridgeshire CB4 9JD

Cheshire
Mr Kenneth A. Paul
Historic Cheshire Churches Trust
Field House
Woodbank Lane
Shotwick
Chester CH1 6JD

Cornwall
Mr Lionel Coates Greenholme
Cornwall Historic Churches Trust
Cambrose
Redruth
Cornwall TR16 4HT

Derbyshire
Mr Alan Bemrose
Derbyshire Historic Churches and
Chapels Trust
1 Greenhill
Wirksworth
Derbyshire DE4 4EN

Devon
J.K.G. Malleson
Devon Historic Churches Trust
Clifford Lodge
Drewsteignton
Devon EX6 6QE

Dorset
Mr Patrick F. Moule
Dorset Historic Churches Trust
Ryalls' Ground
Yetminster
Sherborne
Dorset DT9 6LL

Essex
Mrs Mary Blaxhall
Friends of Essex Churches
Box FEC
Guy Harlings
53 New Street
Chelmsford
Essex CM1 1AT

Gloucestershire
Mr W. J. Eykyn
Gloucestershire Historic Churches Preservation Trust
Abbotts Hill
Duntisbourne Abbotts
Cirencester
Gloucestershire GL7 7JN

Hampshire
Ms Lindie Sawtell
Hampshire and the Islands Historic Churches Trust
20 Oaklands Road
Havant
Hampshire PO9 2RN

Herefordshire
Mrs C. J. A. Gallimore
Herefordshire Historic Churches Trust
The Old Vicarage
Norton Canon
Herefordshire HR4 7BQ

Kent
The Hon Mrs E. Raikes
Friends of Kent Churches
Parsonage Oasts
Yalding
Kent ME18 6HG

Leicestershire
Lay Canon T. Y. Cocks
Leicestershire Historic Churches Trust
24 Beresford Drive
Leicester LE2 3LA

Lincolnshire
Mr R. D. Underwood
Lincolnshire Old Churches Trust
Halfway Farm Cottage
Newark Road
Swinderby
Lincolnshire LN6 9HN

Norfolk
Mr M. Fisher
Norfolk Churches Trust Ltd
9 The Old Church
St Matthew's Road
Norwich
Norfolk NR1 1SP

Northamptonshire
Mr J. A. White MA
Northamptonshire Historic Churches Trust
7 Spencer Parade
Northampton NN1 5AB

Northumbria
The Revd Canon J. E. Ruscoe
Northumbria Historic Churches Trust
The Vicarage
South Hylton
Sunderland
Northumbria SR4 0QB

Nottinghamshire
Mrs Joy Scarrott
Nottinghamshire Historic Churches Trust
38 Manor Close
Edwalton
Nottingham NG12 4BH

Oxfordshire
Mr R. H. Lethbridge
Oxfordshire Historic Churches Trust
The Dower House
Westhall Hill
Fulbrook
Oxfordshire OX18 4BJ

Romney Marsh
Mrs E. A. Marshall
The Romney Marsh Historic Churches Trust
Lansdell House
Rolvenden
Nr Cranbrook
Kent TN17 4LW

Rutland
Mrs L. I. Worall
Rutland Historic Churches Trust
6 Redland Close
Barrowden
Oakham
Rutland LE15 8ES

Shropshire
The Ven. John Hall
Shropshire Historic Churches Trust
The Archdeacon of Salop
Tong Vicarage
Shifnal
Shropshire TF11 8PW

Suffolk
Mr C. K. St J. Bird
Suffolk Churches Preservation Trust
Brinkleys
Hall Street
Long Melford
Suffolk CO10 9JR

Surrey
Mrs N. Osmond
Surrey Churches Preservation Trust
Sylvans
Tilford Road
Farnham
Surrey GU9 8JB

Sussex
Mr Steven Sleight
Sussex Historic Churches Trust
81 Newland Road
Worthing
West Sussex BN11 1LB

Warwickshire and Coventry
Dr Charles Brown
Warwickshire and Coventry
Historic Churches Trust
42 High Street
Warwick CV34 4AS

Wiltshire
Mr J. Caunt
Wiltshire Historic Churches Trust
The Cottage
Barford St Martin
Salisbury
Wiltshire SP3 4AS

Worcester and Dudley
Mr John A. Lakeman
Westlyn Olf Farm
Stockton Road
Abberley
Worcestershire WR6 6AS

Yorkshire
Mr S. R. T. Rowe
Yorkshire Historic Churches Trust
The Old School
Crooked Lane
Kirk Hammerton
Yorkshire YO26 8DG

The County Historic Churches Trusts are all independent charities raising money and helping repair churches and chapels within their own boundaries. They have no financial link with the HCPT, although in many cases the HCPT, the ICBS and the county HCT may help the same church. As well as fund-raising, County Trusts aim to make people more aware of their County's heritage of fine churches. They are also a source of advice and encouragement to hard-pressed parishes.

Index

Other titles published for the Council for the Care of Churches by Church House Publishing:

Church Extensions and Adaptations (£9.95)

Church Floors and Floor Coverings (£3.95)

Church Lighting by Peter Jay and Bill Crawforth (£12.95)

The Churchyards Handbook, 4th edition (£10.95)

The Conservation and Repair of Bells and Bellframes: Code of practice (£6.95)

A Fragile Inheritance: The care of stained glass and historic glazing: a handbook for custodians (£9.95)

A Guide to Church Inspection and Repair (£4.50)

Heating your Church by William Bordass and Colin Bemrose, 3rd edition (£5.95)

Historic Organ Conservation (£9.95)

The Repair and Maintenance of Glass in Churches (£4.50)

Safe and Sound? A guide to church security (£3.50)

Sounds Good: A guide to church organs for incumbents, churchwardens and PCCs (£6.95)

A Stitch in Time: Guidelines for the care of textiles (£2.50)

Stonework: Maintenance and surface repair, 2nd edition (£9.95)

Towards the Conservation and Restoration of Historic Organs: A record of the Liverpool Conference (£9.95)

Widening the Eye of the Needle: Access to church buildings for people with disabilities, 2nd edition (£10.95)

Wildlife in Church and Churchyard, 2nd edition (£9.95)

Wiring your Church (£3.95)